LETTER

K

Ages (5-10)

Kids Colouring Book

Book 13 (Pocket)

By

CHRISELDA BARRETTO

Visit "chriselda.blog"

Contents

FREE GIFT

Thank you so much for buying LETTERS (Japanese - Katakana) – Kids Colouring Book. I know there are loads of amazing colouring books out there, but you chose to spend some time with mine. That's very special. As my way of saying thank you for buying this book, please enjoy my downloadable PDF Bonus filled with images from all of my colouring books. You can colour some of your favorite designs, or sceneries over and over again with this FREE printable file.

Please visit 'chriselda.blog' to download your gift today! Alternatively you could avail of this FREE offer by contacting me at 'chriselda.blog'.

INTRODUCTION

Hi, I am Chriselda; a writer, poet, speaker and an art-lover. I have always loved art…in all of its forms but painting/sketching is the one that resonates with me the most. Through my childhood I remember my mother inscribing me and my sketches for loads of competitions, some of which I won…but it wasn't the prize that interested me but the joy and calm I got from scribbling my personal art on paper!

And then life happened, where I developed my professional skills and spent nearly all of my time growing and working on my career, where I *forgot* about this little gem that I had hidden in my subconscious. Luckily enough, somehow I was given the opportunity to rediscover this latent passion of mine and with it its gentle power of peace and serenity.

Studies are now proving that colouring has the ability to relax the fear center of your brain; the amygdala. It induces the same state as meditating by reducing the thoughts of a restless mind. This generates mindfulness and quietness, which allows your mind to get some rest and calm down.

I have devoted many beautiful, relaxing hours creating my 'Colouring Books For Adults' Series. Recently my six-year-old who loves drawing asked me to make a drawing book for her…I promised her I would! That's where the series of 'Mom…I wanna colour' and 'Letters' - Kids Colouring Books originates from, and I am so happy to share these with all of you! All of the designs, patterns have been hand drawn, and you will find my unique style running through all of them! Let the kids enjoy many fun, calm hours colouring and learning. In the '*LETTERS - Japanese*' books, the kids will practice writing Japanese letters and they can colour them too!

Join me in spreading some positive, happy and peaceful vibes but most importantly 'Let the kids have some colouring fun!'

What makes Letters (Japanese) colouring book unique:
- A first of its kind colouring book introducing kids to a foreign language
- It incorporates learning into fun
- All the letter illustrations are done by hand
- Unique hand drawn patterns
- Dashed-lined letters helping kids to trace on
- Letters with accompanying arrows, showing how to write each letter

TEST PAGE

This page is the perfect place to test your materials and colours before you start working on the actual designs.

KATAKANA

ア a	イ i	ウ u	エ e	オ o
カ ka	キ ki	ク ku	ケ ke	コ ko
サ sa	シ shi	ス su	セ se	ソ so
タ ta	チ chi	ツ tsu	テ tse	ト to
ナ na	ニ ni	ヌ nu	ネ ne	ノ no
ハ ha	ヒ hi	フ fu	ヘ he	ホ ho
マ ma	ミ mi	ム mu	メ me	モ mo
ヤ ya		ユ yu		ヨ yo
ラ ra	リ ri	ル ru	レ re	ロ ro
ワ wa	ヰ wi		ヱ we	ヲ wo
	ン n			

a

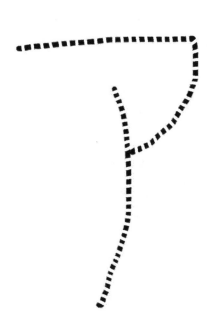

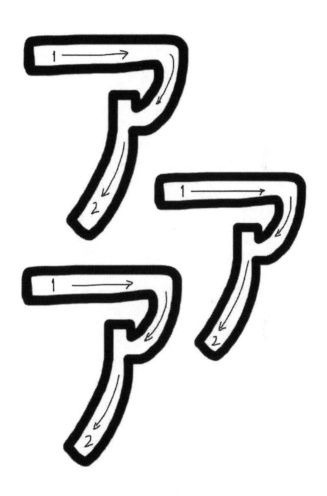

i

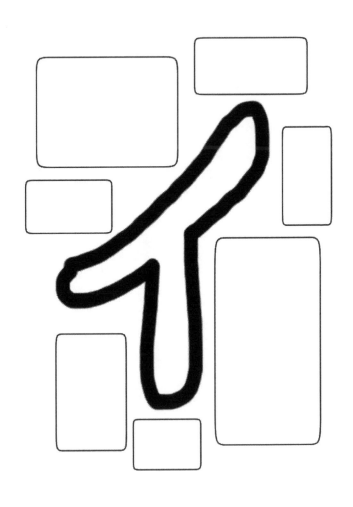

u

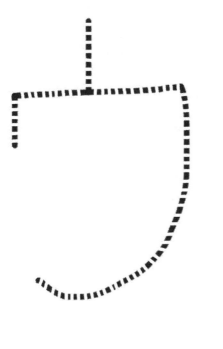

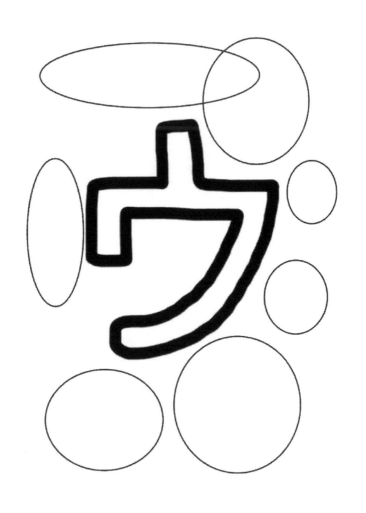

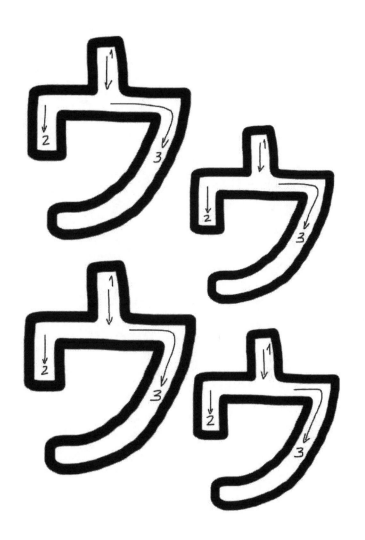

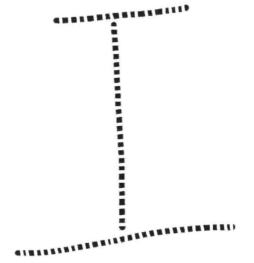

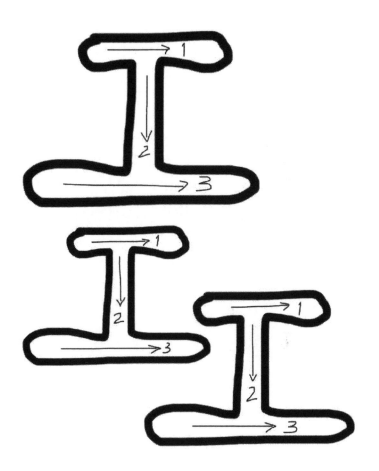

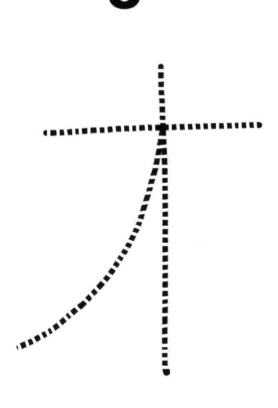

ka

ki

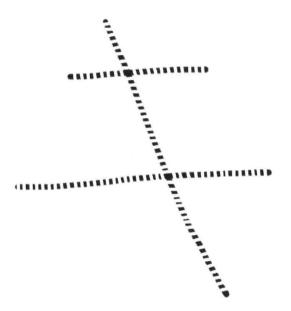

ku

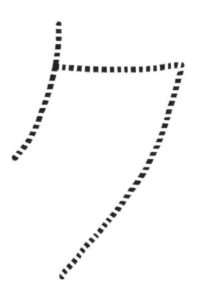

ke

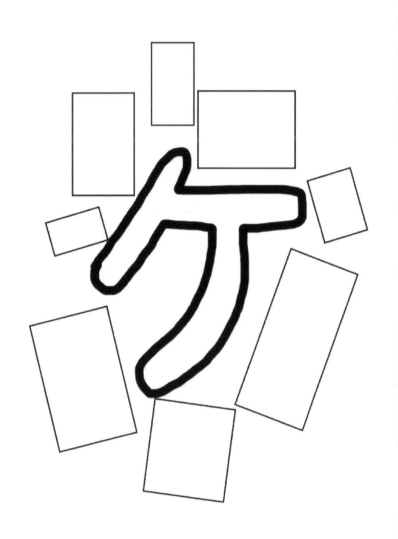

ko

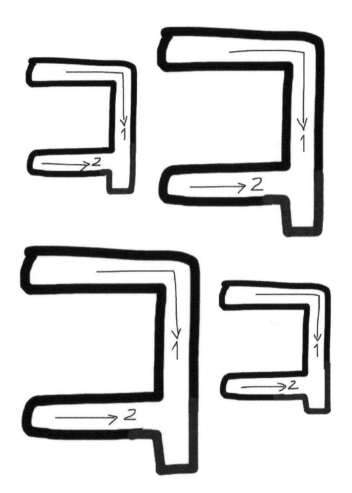

sa

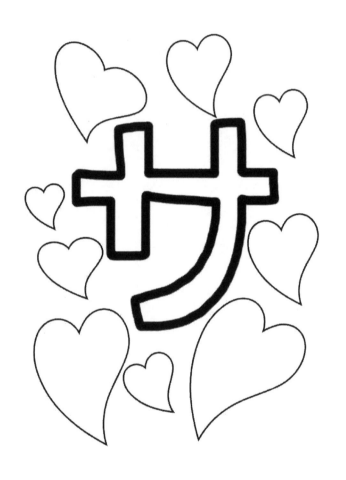

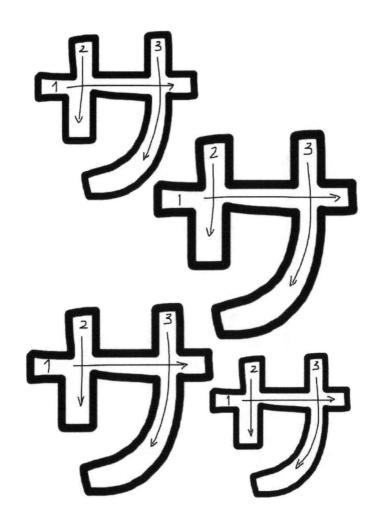

shi

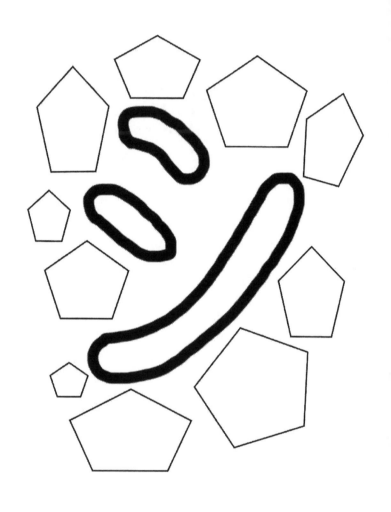

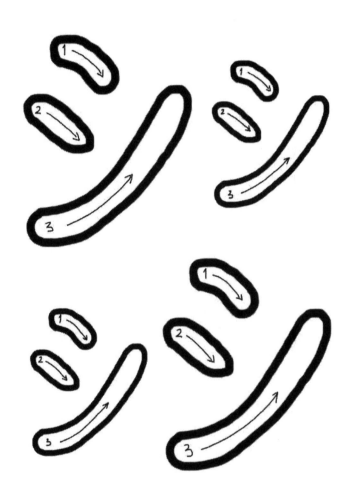

su

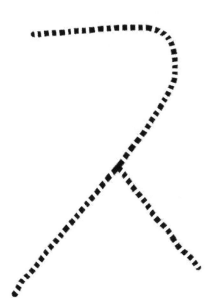

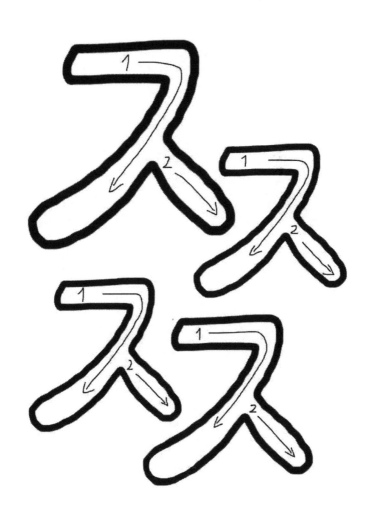

se

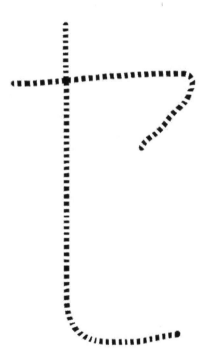

so

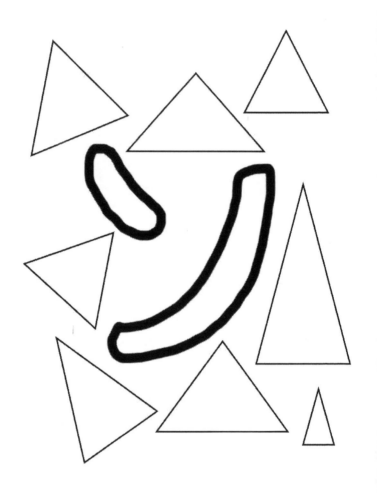

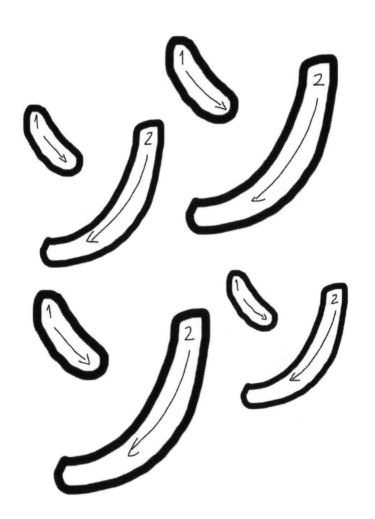

ta

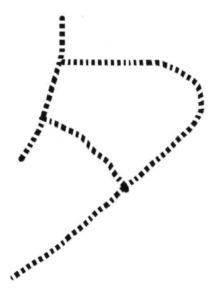

chi

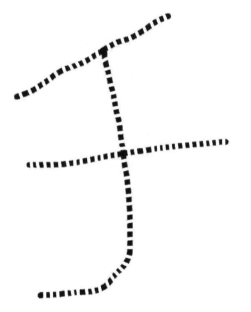

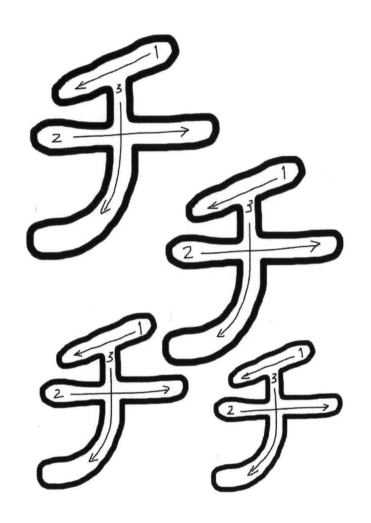

tsu

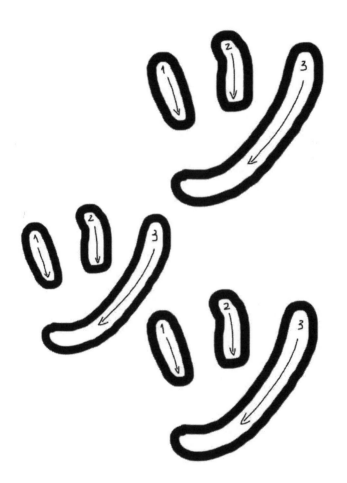

tse

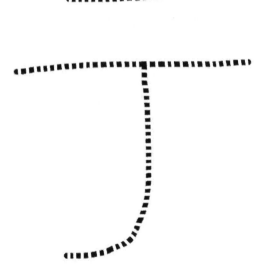

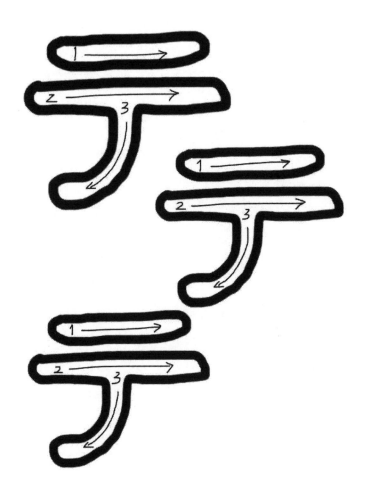

to

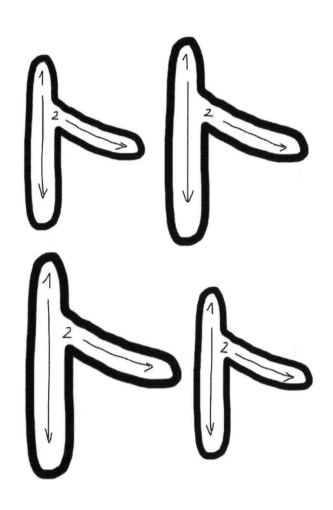

na

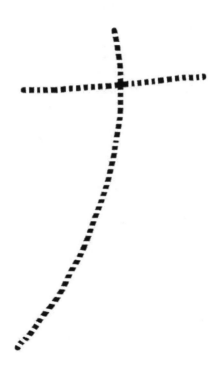

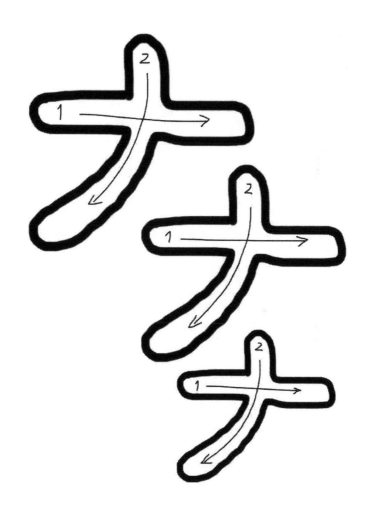

ni

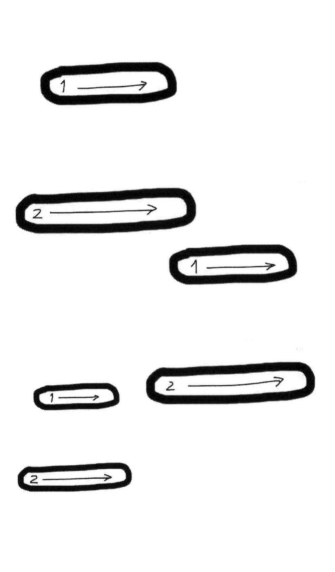

nu

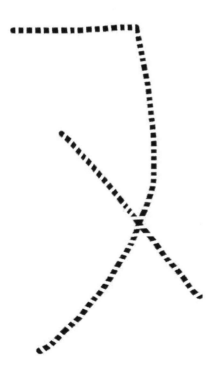

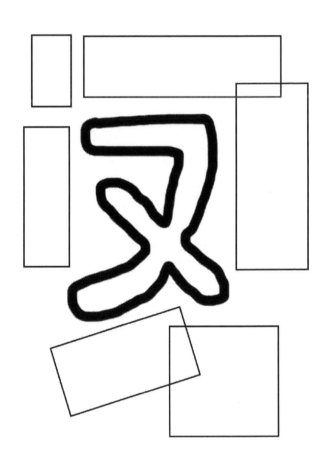

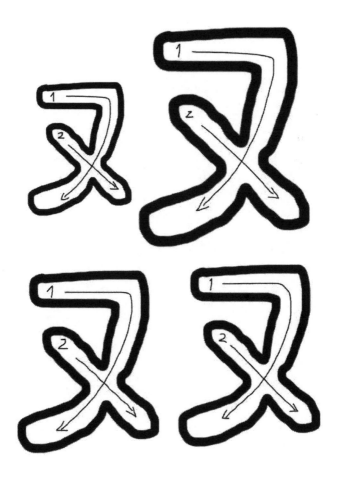

ne

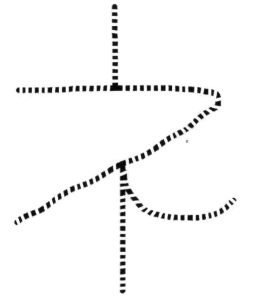

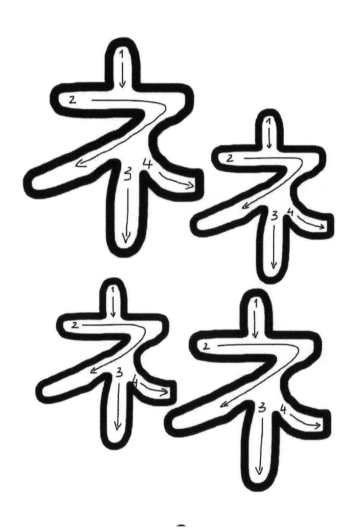

no

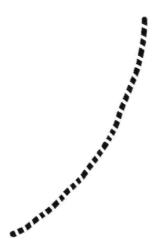

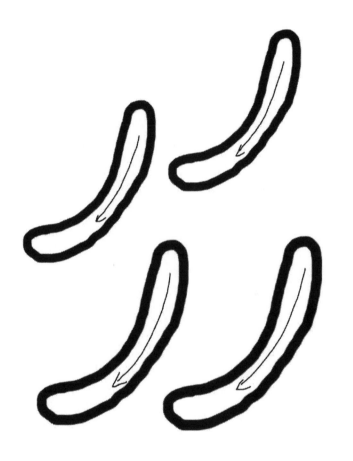

ha

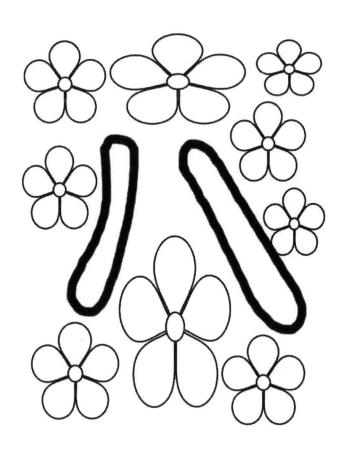

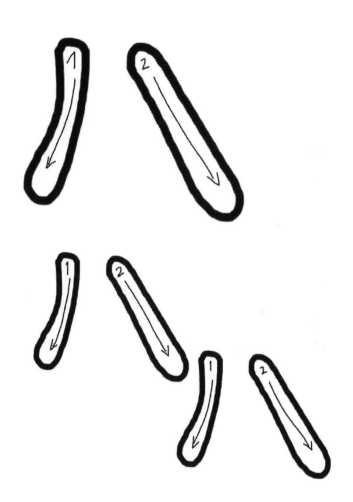

hi

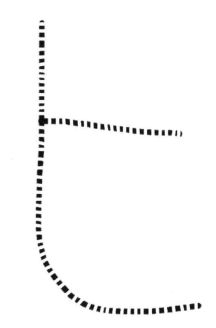

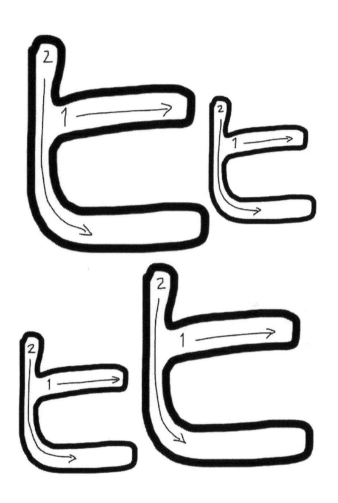

fu

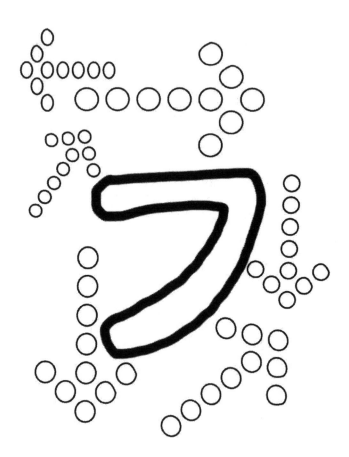

ラブ

he

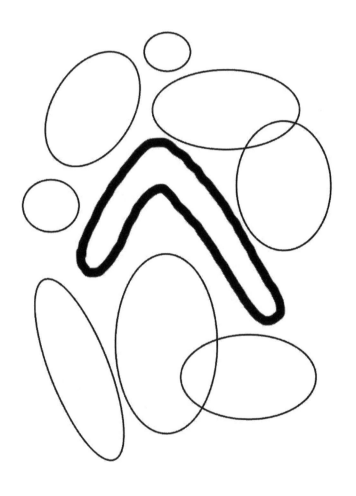

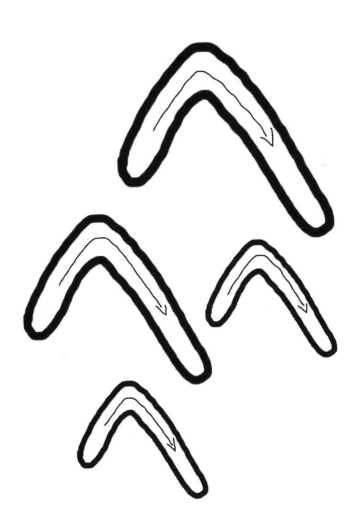

ho

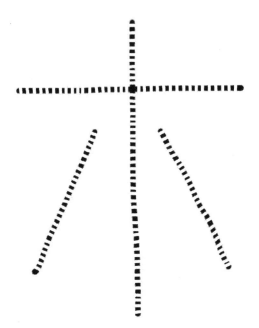

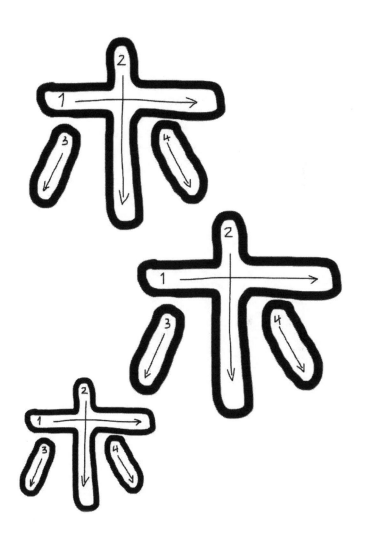

ma

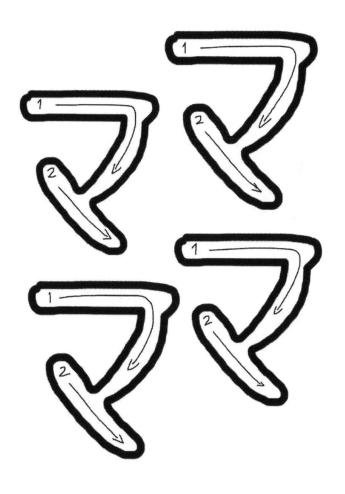

mi

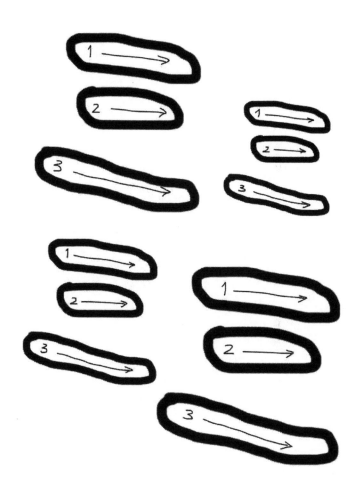

mu

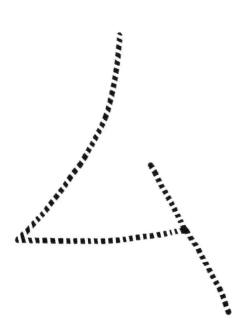

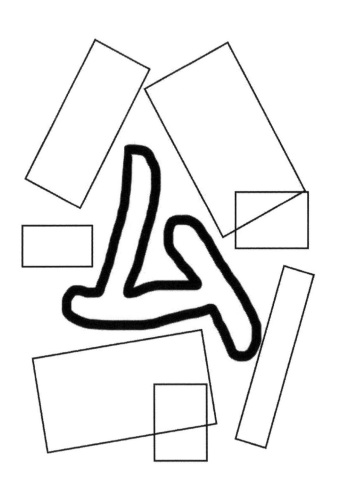

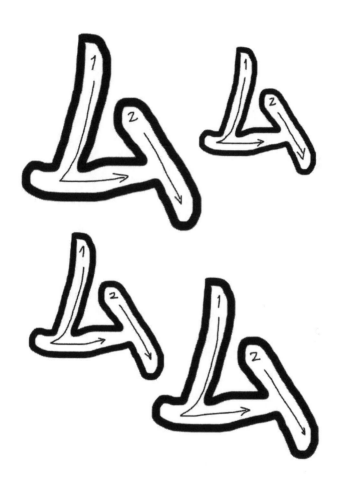

me

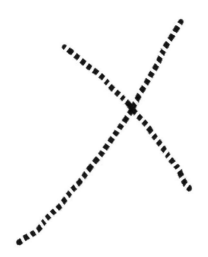

mo

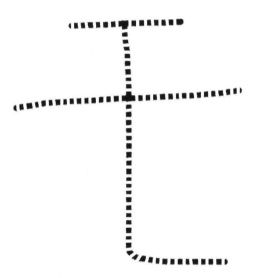

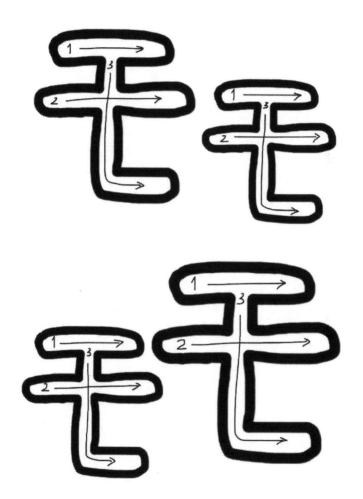

ya

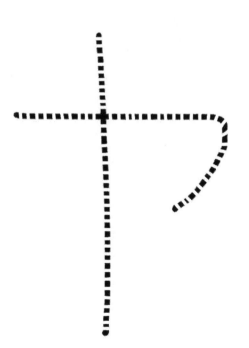

yu

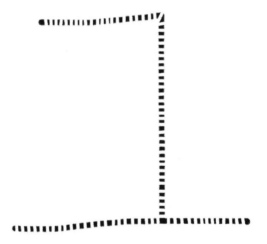

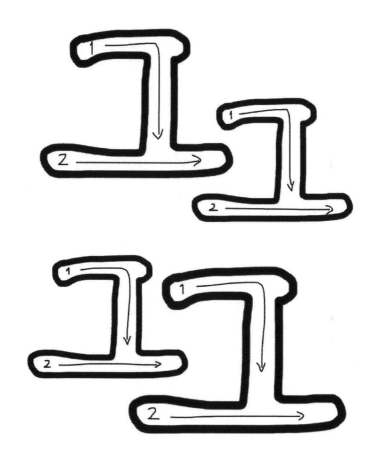

yo

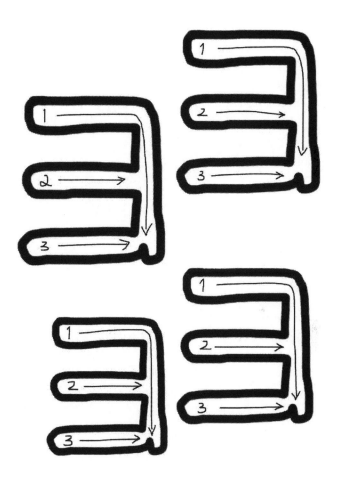

ra

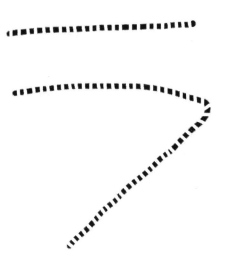

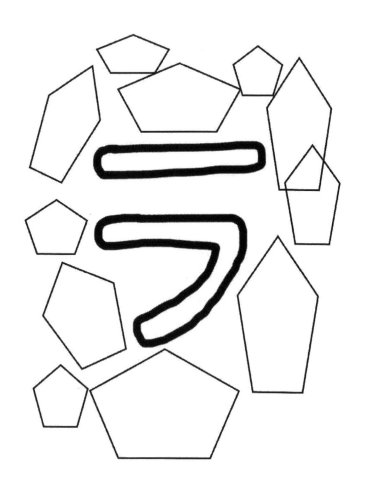

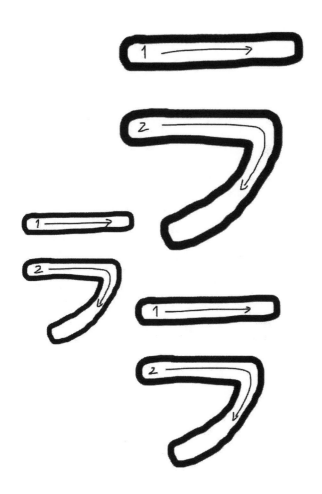

ri

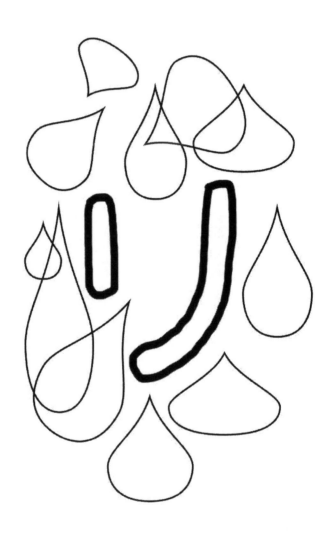

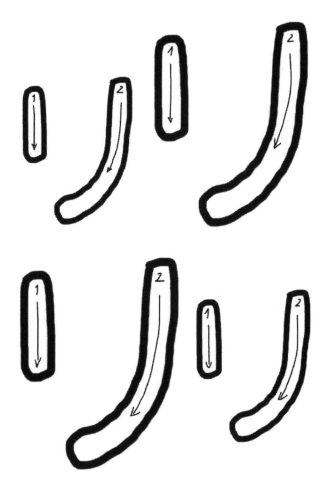

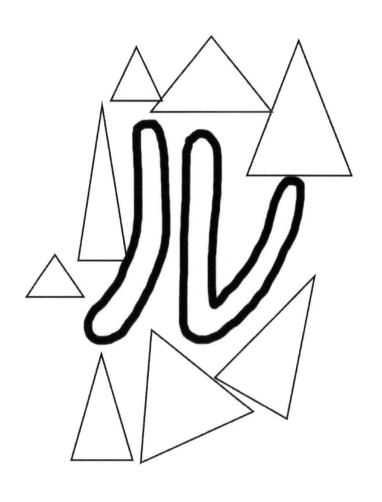

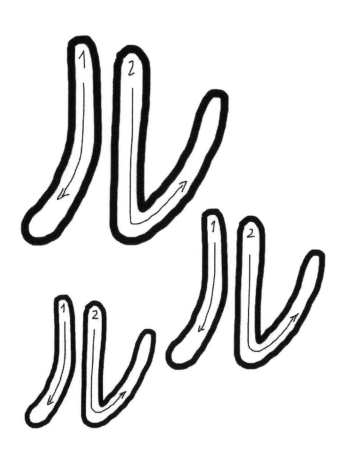

re

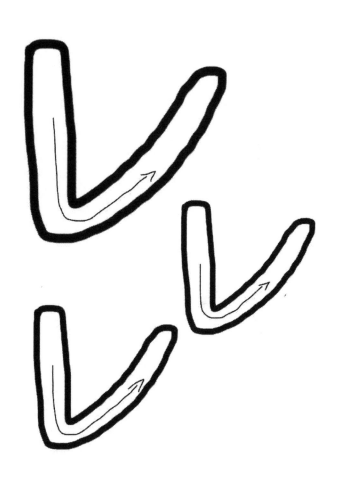

ro

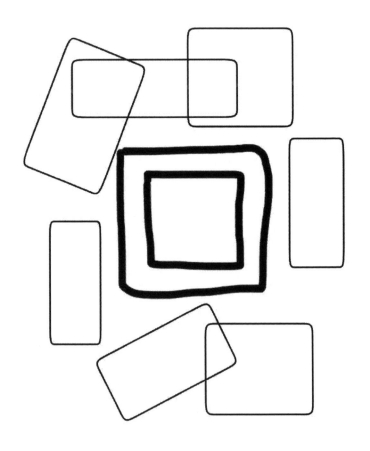

wa

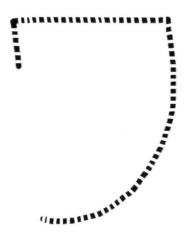

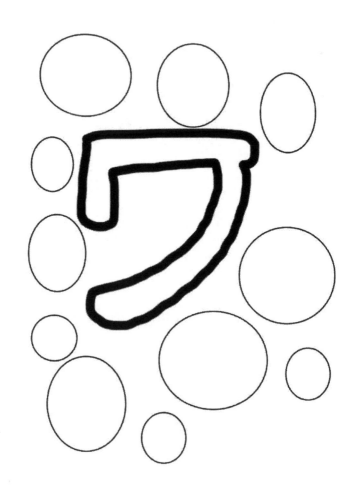

wi

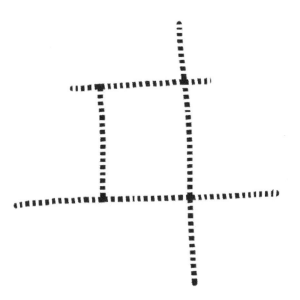

we

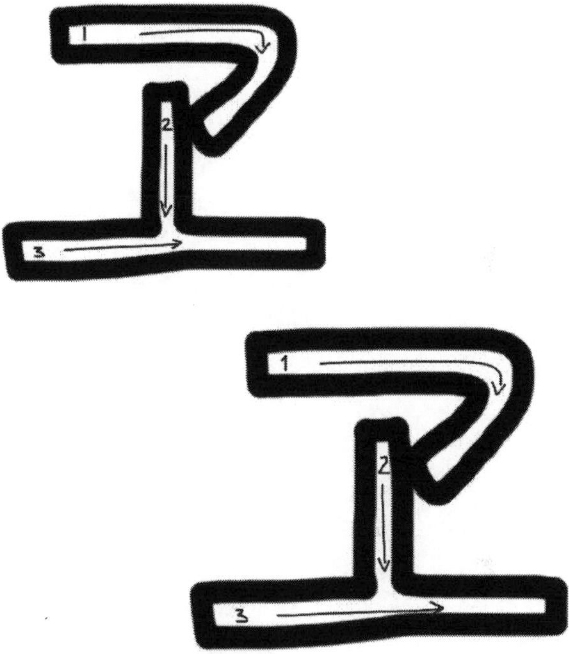
1
2
3
1
2
3
1
2
3

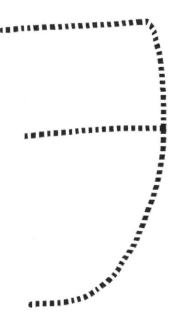

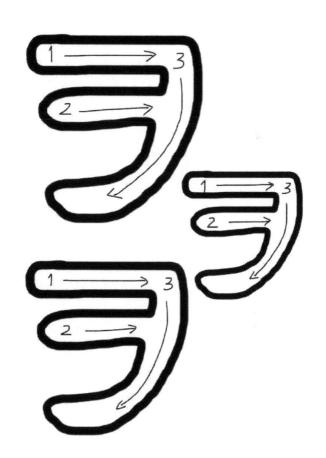

n

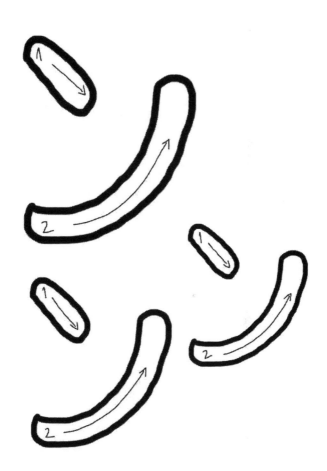

ABOUT THE AUTHOR

Chriselda, a multi-genre, prolific author and speaker, with a background in Business Administration and Chemistry/Microbiology lives in Belgium. She also hosts the Podcast – The 3 Pillars and is the creator of ART-IS-IN, The Dig and her blog 'chriselda.blog'

Having traveled the world extensively, as an Inflight Safety Training Instructor, she has worked in the Aviation industry for nearly two decades.

Always with a touch of artistic creativity along with being an ex-professional modern jazz dancer, she loves music and is passionate about writing! She speaks 5 languages & writes poetry, stories and quotes. She has published more than 30 books, from which over 13 belong to her 'Colouring Books For Adults' Series!

Her writing covers fiction and non-fiction, with the likes of poetry, horror, thriller, romance, supernatural, children's illustration, but she enjoys telling a story in narrative poetry the most!

Currently she has a lot of things going on; launching her healing jewelry collection – 'Hand Made by Chriselda B', airing her podcast, interviewing artists, producing her tutorial series, creating more colouring books, not only for adults but also for children and she is working on her Self-help/Image-Building Book, that she had first started on her blog: 'chriselda.blog'

Being a qualified Life Coach and Motivational Speaker, she also practices NLP and Mindfulness. Aiming to share her knowledge and experience, she is a speaker on many topics ranging from Creative Writing, Personal Development, Aerotoxic Syndrome to Aviation Safety and Self-Publishing. She is a certified Holistic Counsellor & a Reiki and Aura and Chakra Healer.

ALSO BY CHRISELDA BARRETTO

STAND-ALONE:

UN/CENTERED

ENIGMA

SHORTER

DREAMS & DEW

COFFEE & BAGELS

SHE SAID!

ACCURSED FOREST

AVIATION STORIES-1 : DYING TO FLY

THE ULTIMATE COLLECTION OF MILLENNIAL QUOTES

MUST LOVE POETRY

CHILDRENS BOOKS

MELINA'S RAINBOW

MELINA'S REGENBOOG (DUTCH EDITION)

SERIES:

THE CREEP SERIES:

THE CREEP - 1

THE CREEP REVEALED – 2

COLOURING BOOKS FOR ADULTS SERIES:

BOOK 1 - ABSTRACTS

BOOK 2 - FASHION STATEMENTS

BOOK 3 - SCENERIES

BOOK 4 - CHRISTMASSY

BOOK 5 - MUDRAS

BOOK 6 - YOGA

BOOK 7 - MOVEMENT

BOOK 8 - MANDALAS AND PATTERNS

BOOK 9 - SPACE AND SATELLITES

BOOK 10 - GEOMETRY

BOOK 11 - FACE GRIDS

BOOK 12 - DIVINITIES

BOOK 13 - AFFIRMED

BOOK 14 - LINE ART

BOOK 15 - HALLOWEEN

KIDS COLOURING BOOKS SERIES:

BOOK 1 - ANIMALS

BOOK 2 - CAPITAL LETTERS

BOOK 3 - SMALL LETTERS

BOOK 4 - CAPITAL LETTERS – GREEK

BOOK 5 - SMALL LETTERS - GREEK

BOOK 6 - CAPITAL LETTERS – GREEK [Pocket]

BOOK 7 - SMALL LETTERS – GREEK [Pocket]

BOOK 8 - LETTERS – HINDI

BOOK 9 - LETTERS – HINDI [Pocket]

BOOK 10 - LETTERS – JAPANESE - Hiragana

BOOK 11 - LETTERS – JAPANESE – Hiragana [Pocket]

Find all her books @ Amazon and 'chriselda.blog'